NATURALLY AGED NOSTALGIA

NATURALLY AGED NOSTALGIA
Volume II
More Fun Stories for Spirited Seniors

By John C. Liburdi

This book is dedicated to U.S. Air Force Missileer crews serving in underground Launch Control Centers located in remote areas of the country. Nuclear and Missile Operations Officers constitute a highly dedicated cadre of superior military professionals. They remain vigilant on a "24/7/365" basis to safeguard our nation. Their creed is: To Deter and Assure

- CONTENTS -

INTRODUCTION

Naturally Aged Nostalgia (Volume II) is a fun book that intentionally violates the timeless axiom: Some things are better left unsaid. Readers are encouraged to savor the humor and irony as they read each story. No one should be taken aback by what's expressed in jest. The sole intent of this book is to poke fun at our tumultuous planet, and America's frazzled senior citizens are being given front row seats to enjoy that entertaining spectacle.

In days gone by, the average American's living and working domain was pretty much limited to the borders of hometown USA. Naturally, that helped facilitate a sense of order in our lives. But then we began to be influenced and impacted by global forces emanating from far beyond where we live, thus spawning a multitude of changes that have already gone too far and run too deep. Obviously, there's no way to turn back the hands of time to bring our crazy world back to its normal state.

The global evolution has changed our daily lives in many ways; furthermore, the pace of change keeps accelerating with the passage of time. Of course, there's both a positive side and a negative side to all this, so we dare not lament too hard. But as we reluctantly embrace our nebulous future, somewhere deep inside our hearts we have residual feelings for what's been left behind. This book revives and rekindles some of that warm nostalgia, to be enjoyed once again.

Most of us can remember befriending our neighbors, hearing a brat get a spanking, buying penny candy, proudly washing our cars by hand, respectfully asking elders for advice, receiving milk deliveries at home, chatting with the hardware store owner, setting up board games, and hanging laundry in the fresh outdoors. Plus, back then, we all could easily relate to Norman Rockwell's illustrations on glossy covers of *The Saturday Evening Post*. Much of that was abandoned as we seniors were forcibly thrust into the future.

Today, the Internet is the preferred source of friendship; spanking a naughty child is a felony; candy bars cost a buck; cars are washed with a credit card; old people are often treated as excess baggage; dairy products are sold at gas stations; former hardware store owners work at Walmart; board games are played on smartphones, and outdoor clotheslines violate homeowner association rules. Plus, many time-honored magazines have either faded away or migrated to the Internet.

Smooth talking politicians and ruthless businessmen would have us believe that the old ways were bad and what they offer is good. They bore into our minds, coercing us into adopting practices and buying products just to increase their power and wealth. Sadly, those trusted "leaders" gutted the economy and it collapsed around our ears. Now senior citizens celebrate their austere retirements with generic beer while corporate executives celebrate their "golden parachute" retirements with vintage champagne.

At this juncture, we don't really have much leverage in determining our own fate as our morphing world bounces along through time and space. So in the end, it's pointless to become too cynical or bitter about all the inevitable changes; again, most of them do have both pluses and minuses. Still, there surely must be some graceful and comfortable way to live through all this global transformation.

Perhaps instead of becoming "future shock" victims, America's senior citizens should reclaim their dignity and rediscover happiness. One way ahead would be to expose the absurdity and find the humor in this upside down world; that would at least allow seniors to lay claim to the proverbial last laugh. Hopefully, that's what readers will get out of this book: a chance to cherish the past, revel in truth and, most importantly, enjoy some humor.

Indeed, it's often been said that laughter is the best medicine. That prescription becomes a more potent remedy when it's laced with a touch of vengeance. Even though that's an addictive potion, please feel free to savor as much as you wish by reading these short stories. Doctor Andy Rooney would certainly approve!

CHAPTER 1

Oldsters Will Save the Nation!

Recent cyber attacks by Russia and other countries have proven to be a wake-up call for America. It's now widely understood and accepted that our nation's entire computer-based infrastructure is vulnerable to hostile attacks, and it's extremely difficult to defend against them. The global Internet is actually the foundation upon which our global society and global economy stand. Today, all countries are so interconnected and interdependent that we can't simply unplug from worldwide networks as a defense measure.

So, what's our expected fate if "Geek" terrorists launch a cyber attack and shut down the national infrastructure? Much of Generation X and the entire Millennium generation will go into severe culture shock. With the loss of the Internet and computers, they'll become zombies, wandering around streets littered with discarded smartphones and computer tablets. It will be up to senior citizens across the country to jump-start the nation and get it back on its feet. They're the ones who were living a sensible lifestyle until younger generations sold our collective souls to computer tycoons like Bill Gates and Steve Jobs.

First, seniors will have to mentor young people on the traditional ways of traveling from point A to point B. Modern automobiles will shut down as viruses ruin their imbedded computer systems. So, elders will have to teach younger folks how to drive old cars imported from Cuba. With no GPS navigation systems available, every gas station will need a senior citizen on staff to teach the art of folding paper maps. Also, airplanes that rely on "fly-by-wire" computer systems will be grounded; thus, trains will become the primary mode of long-distance travel. Millions of riders will need to be tutored on train schedule interpretation and sleeper car etiquette.

Obviously, oldsters all know how to conduct business, even without computers. ATM machines will be out of service and credit cards won't work anymore; thus, thousands of bank tellers will be called out of retirement to meet the overwhelming demand for big wads of paper money. One can also expect that the inability to shop on-line will bring back the mom and pop stores of yesteryear. The loss of the Internet, cable

TV and radio stations will also drive big changes in advertising. Spam will once again be just something to eat, and armies of old folks will take to the streets, adorned with sandwich board advertisements.

Necessary changes in education will shock the academic community to its "Common Core." Without the ability to Google for information, the old door-to-door encyclopedia sales force will rise again. Elderly teachers will be showing students how to solve math problems using vintage slide rules rather than math Apps on computers and smart tablets. And with the loss of e-mail capability, computer keyboards will be rendered useless; thus, kids will have to learn how to handwrite letters—activity that might even make the Postal Service a self-sustaining enterprise!

The family structure will necessarily change in many homes. Previously ignored grandparents will be lured back home to live with their kids. Yes, it's always nice to have loving grandmas around, but there's an ulterior motive in this case. There'll be no electricity to run washing machines, vacuum cleaners, dishwashers, kitchen mixers, etc. Who better than highly experienced grannies to deal with all the housekeeping chores in the manual mode? Grandpas will stay busy feeding and training vicious "hired gun" dogs that replace defunct home alarm systems.

Social relationships will see dramatic change too. Facebook friends will be gone forever; so, grandmas will have to demonstrate how to coffee klatch with nearby neighbors that the kids never wanted to meet. Family photos stored in the Internet "cloud" will also be permanently lost. As a result, antique shops will experience a huge demand for conventional cameras and—once film becomes available again—grandpas will teach kids how to manually focus a camera. On-line computer games will no longer be accessible; so, dusty Parcheesi and Monopoly board games will be brought down from attics for families to enjoy.

Yes, whenever the big cyber attack occurs, it'll be back-to-basics for quite some time. Drafting elderly people into public service will be the only way to save our nation, and retirement homes will become the cultural and learning centers of America. Most senior citizens won't be able to resist uttering the occasional "I told you so," which is certainly a small price to pay for all the good they'll be doing. Of course, it remains to be seen if younger generations will be humble and respectful enough to accept that mild rebuke.

CHAPTER 2

Old Time TV News Was Good News

There's little doubt that long-gone TV news icons like Water Cronkite and his contemporaries are perpetually spinning in their respective graves as modern-day 24/7 cable news permeates homes all over America. Those old guys had the right formula: objective news without zany theatrics and mind games. Furthermore, they let me know what was going on in the world without trying to shove my face deep into each and every overseas toilet bowl.

Back in the late fifties and early sixties, it was easy to tell when the evening news came on TV because I'd hear solemn music mixed with noisy Teletype machine clatter or urgent Morse code beeping. Then a stern a newscaster would give all of America a perfunctory greeting followed by a series of brief news items, each one providing just the key essentials and known facts of a given situation. While reading the news, they'd often display easy to view photos or film clips—devoid of any blood and guts.

Another appealing aspect of the old news was that there were very few commercials, and those ads usually portrayed happy people having lots of fun together. Like cheery folks "Seeing the USA in a Chevrolet" or perhaps a smiley family sitting at the kitchen table, enjoying some "Mmmm Mmmm Good" soup. Those uplifting moments took the edge off any psychological distress caused by the news, thereby preventing the onset of depression.

On the other hand, today's news often starts with ear-splitting rock music and cutting-edge graphics to mesmerize TV viewers. Then the cameraman pans a studio equipped with futuristic furniture, absent of any equipment that would even hint at newsgathering activity. The focal points are clear glass desks and very low couches intended to facilitate provocative views of long-legged, bleached-blond news divas. And some news broadcasts even feature groups of trendy blabbermouths spewing out their unqualified opinions followed by silly laughter.

Of course, today's evening news format mandates at least four commercials in between each news item.

The TV commercials highlight every malady known to medical science and offer pleasurable cures in luxurious settings. Then comes the usual litany of repulsive side effects, with a warning to quickly see a doctor if death occurs while taking the medication. That's all followed by timely ads for "ambulance-chaser" law firms. But it's not all gloom and doom; romantic couples portray how magical pills can transform burnt out old men into virile gigolos.

Our world is now saturated with video cameras and surrounded by orbiting satellites that enhance news coverage. This allows us to experience all the global carnage via real-time TV, horribly graphic views of bloody warfare, fatal shootings and tragic crashes. Oh, don't forget the satellite links to insensitive reporters that interview grieving families at crash sites: "How do you feel about your mother being killed in the plane crash? Do you suspect the pilot was drunk? Will you get much money from the lawsuit against the airline?"

Admittedly, Ted Turner's creation of a global satellite network for TV news was a spectacular feat. However, he should have made it a one-way mirror, in our favor! Newscasters here eagerly exercise their Freedom of Speech to display America's dirty laundry to the world via live TV—O.J. cruising around L.A in his SUV, Bill testifying about grayish sexual activity with Monica, etc. And what about the disclosure of sensitive military information via global TV news? Security leaks were treasonous acts back in the day; today they're merely "oops" scenarios in the context of infotainment.

Yep, the old TV news was decidedly better. Newscasters of that era had rock-solid character, much like a town mayor or church minister. Cronkite, Swayze, Huntley and Brinkley dispassionately reported cold facts about a train derailment on the other side of the country or a bank robbery in some faraway town. And they'd allow just a few delightful commercial breaks to reassure me that, no matter what, my daily life was still going to be filled with bliss.

Most of those TV newscasters appearing on yesteryear's black and white TVs weren't pretty to look at, but they did a pretty darn good job of reporting the news in thirty short minutes. Afterwards, they kept the world in check so that I could get on with my life as though nothing bad had ever happened anywhere. Yes indeed, I felt truly at peace each time I heard Mr. Cronkite's closing declaration each evening: "And that's the way it is."

CHAPTER 3

Aging Minds Are Getting Smarter

A few decades ago, senior citizens used to retire from mundane cradle-to-grave jobs and then languish as they sat in their rocking chairs on front porches. They'd watch the world go by from that that vantage point, all the while sipping discount liquor or convenience store wine in a vain effort to keep their memories refreshed. Wow, quality of life has sure improved for us contemporary seniors; we're getting smarter as we grow older!

Not surprisingly, health care managers would attribute our improved intellects to specialized medicine and therapy. We're encouraged to eat slimy jellyfish residue and chunks of magnesium to boost our brainpower. Then they challenge us with baffling mind games to activate our brain cells. And if those methods don't energize the cognitive process, the Docs eagerly resort to electronic and magnetic stimulation therapy to light up our craniums.

Myself, I'm convinced that daily life has become so complex that just living it is enough to keep our brains running on all cylinders. Nothing is simple anymore, and average citizens struggle to keep up with generation after generation of short-lived technology— usually a three-year or less life cycle. As we master one generation, the next evolution is already upon us. But embracing all that new technology is what allows us to remain in the fast lane of society's rat race.

Our cars used to have a simple shift lever on the steering column and chrome knobs for each individual function. Now car interiors resemble the Starship Enterprise, with two paddle shifters and control buttons all over the steering wheel, plus one or two touch-screen video displays on the dashboard. These days, you have to be one smart cookie to get from point A to point B.

In yesteryear, doing the laundry involved a tub washing machine with a ringer that squeezed out some of the water before the wet laundry was hauled outdoors to the clothesline. Now we carefully program the laundry machines' imbedded computers in order to do the load, hopefully without shrinking the clothes to doll size. Likewise, we've all had to master the tricky microwave oven controls—not all food cooks on the popcorn setting. Yep, operating today's household appliances involves plenty of mental exercise.

Some of us even remember getting up from the armchair to physically change TV channels by twisting a big knob, channel by channel. Now we juggle two or three remote controls to "manage" our multi-component entertainment systems. It's so complicated that big-box stores send "Geeks" to our homes to train us on how to operate the equipment, which is now also fed programing via the Internet where black-and-white TV reruns of *I Love Lucy* and *The Honeymooners* are stored.

Back in the day, we used to take pen and paper in hand to scribe letters to our friends and sweethearts. Indeed, some of those perfumed love letters are probably preserved in trunks up in our attics. Today, we seniors launch public tweets and post regrettable comments and photos on Facebook for the world to view. Then we enjoy Skype or FaceTime video sessions with grandkids on our high tech devices—how clever of us!

Remember when our neighborhoods were so safe that we left the doors to our homes unlocked and kept spending cash in a jar on a kitchen shelf? Now we set up complicated alarm systems to defend our homes and protect valuables, requiring that we memorize numeric codes and passwords to activate an electronic defense perimeter each evening. Add to that all the constantly changing passwords we have to memorize for Internet banking and on-line shopping!

So, it's obvious that we've become smarter over the years. For example, now I'm smart enough to know that e-mails asking me to click on a link and then log in to verify my bank account password are just phishing attempts to steal my money. I'm also smart enough to know that telephonic threats from the IRS to sue me if I don't immediately pay a hefty fine are bogus. Plus, I'm smart enough to know that there's no such thing as a free lunch even though dapper financial advisors keep mailing me tickets for free steak dinners.

More importantly, I've become smart enough to suspect that the obscene e-mails I keep receiving from foreign girls with exotic names like Natasha, Sabrina and Li-Mei aren't sincere invitations to establish an amorous relationship. Sadly, those alluring e-mails are probably just some kind of scam. Hmmm, my healthy brain notwithstanding, perhaps in this case there's some merit to the old adage "Ignorance is bliss." Hey, just saying…

CHAPTER 4

Pricilla's Passion for Pricey Purses

My wife Pricilla is a pretty wonderful old gal. However, despite her many admirable qualities, she does have one serious flaw: an obsession with purses. Much like the former First Lady of the Philippines who once owned three thousand pairs of shoes, Pricilla is endeavoring to achieve a similar level of success, but in terms of purses collected.

Pricilla loves all kinds of purses, although she favors those made of luxurious leather. Her desire for any given purse is directly proportional to its price—the more expensive the better. She spends a great deal of time shopping for purses, either in purse boutiques or in the accessories area of department stores, mostly in the section where designer purses are kept under lock and key.

I never really gave purses much thought until I saw comedienne Ruth Buzzi—as a homely spinster—use a long strapped purse to whack insulting men on the *Laugh-in* TV show, and also some cocky guys in one of Dean Martin's celebrity roasts. I suppose the purse has evolved since that time—more sophistication, more variety and higher prices.

Interestingly, some owners use the purse to defend themselves. Initially, it was simply placing a brick inside a purse and then wielding it as a skull-busting weapon. Then came the clever idea that's often portrayed in comedies: placing a rattrap inside the purse so thieves suffer instant justice. Next came pepper spray; just reach into the stylish leather armory for an aerosol can and start inflicting pain. Today, some purses even have built-in shields to defend against electronic pickpockets who try to remotely read data off of credit card chips.

Anyhow, I once pressed my luck by telling Pricilla that a woman's purse is considered to be an extremely filthy place, filled with dirt and germs. She instantly transformed my observation into a valid rationale for going out and buying more new purses. That left me rather depressed until the day she foolishly put a few chocolate bars inside a purse that was resting in the hot sunshine. Her truly catastrophic event proved to be one refreshing "I told you so" scenario for me.

Pricilla is the queen of purses. Her subjects include those in her court (purses in her glass display case), those locked in dungeons (purses waiting in closets), and then the unfortunate ones banished from her realm (purses stored in the attic). Speaking of fortune, there's an old tradition of placing a penny in a new purse to bring the bearer good luck. Today, the same level of luck requires a Krugerrand gold coin. Nevertheless, I myself enjoyed a bit of good luck while probing Pricilla's old purses in the attic.

In the effort to instantly divorce herself from purses no longer in her favor, Pricilla would hastily stow them in the attic. She would inevitably forget to check the many pockets, thus leaving a significant amount of folding money and loose change in the purses. My discovery of her frequent oversight allowed me to amass quite a sum of cash over the years. With that money in hand, I recently purchased the ultimate Baby Boomer dream machine: a new Harley Davidson motorcycle.

I was struggling to come up with a safe strategy for bringing the Harley home without facing Pricilla's wrath, and maybe the third-degree to learn how I obtained the money for this big purchase. Well, I threw caution to the wind and simply drove the Harley home while she was out shopping for some new purses. While nervously awaiting Pricilla's return, I suddenly heard our remotely controlled garage door start to open; obviously, she was approaching the house. Oh brother, it's time to go out and face the music.

Pricilla pulled into the driveway and saw the brand new Harley parked in the middle of the garage. I could see her eyes nearly bulge out of their sockets, and I read her lips saying, "What the hell?" But her expression suddenly changed as she stepped out of the car; I actually saw a smile of delight on her face. Then I noticed that her gaze was fixed on the motorcycle's beautiful deluxe leather saddlebags.

Pricilla walked over and ran her hand across one of them, caressing the leather and admiring the fringe. I had to steady myself as I heard her say, "These are gorgeous leather saddlebags! How about we ride this Harley to Sunday church service; people there will be green with envy when they see these expensive saddlebags!" I enthusiastically replied, "Oh yes, by all means dear."

Then, in her euphoric state, Pricilla suggested that I also buy a Gucci men's shoulder bag to wear on Sundays. Hmmm, in this delicate situation, spending a grand or two on a man purse seems to make good sense—right?

CHAPTER 5

Humans Are Becoming Obsolete

Although I'm not known to be a gregarious person, interaction with my fellow human beings is something I've always enjoyed. Sadly, there seem to be fewer and fewer opportunities to converse with humans. That's because they've been removed from so many services and processes. It seems that many of us are becoming obsolete.

In my past travels, it was always reassuring to know that a street-smart taxi driver would pick me up at the airport and help me get oriented to the city. Those friendly chaps with heavy foreign accents always gave me the weather forecast, great restaurant recommendations and some shopping tips. With the advent of driverless cars, I'm going to have lonely taxi rides and no guides to help me get my bearings.

I remember the long gone elevator boy in my office building. The look on his face as I got on the elevator each morning told me if there was a spot on my tie or if my fly was unzipped, or even reassured me that I was looking good enough to impress my colleagues and the boss. My invaluable critic has been replaced by a digitized voice announcement that communicates nothing to me except the floor number.

What about those nice UPS and FedEx guys who deliver packages? Their days are numbered now that Amazon is delivering packages via unmanned aerial vehicles; plus, Dominos has started delivering pizzas the same way. Not only do I miss interacting with those fine chaps, I'm also left with the perplexing issue: Should I tip the pizza delivery drone as much as I gave the pizza delivery guy?

These days, some doctors are living by a cutting-edge version of the Hippocratic oath. Rather than get their hands all bloody and risk malpractice lawsuits, surgeons have turned over their most critical work to mechanical robots. Robotic surgery might be an OK thing if the Docs would at least remotely oversee the operation while they're flirting with nurses in the ward breakroom.

Then we've got a few chain restaurants that don't let waitresses do anything but haul food and beverages. The tablet computers on each table force you to communicate your order directly to the kitchen and to pay for your meal by swiping your credit card on the side of the tablet, including a nice tip for the server who has stayed silently in the background throughout your entire dining experience.

Just announced in the news is the new air traffic control system, run autonomously by collision avoidance computers that tell aircraft what altitude and heading they should fly. Soon we'll no longer have coffee drinking, chain smoking air traffic controllers in the tower. Their muffled voices giving unintelligible navigation instructions via crackly radio transmissions will be sorely missed.

Another place where humans are dropping out of the picture is the factory. Robots are taking over manufacturing plants. So, that's fewer workers swearing at each other on the assembly lines and less gossiping in lunchrooms. Eventually, boisterous union meetings and picket lines will also become a thing of the past; that means no more hostile employees for TV news reporters to interview.

Of course, we shouldn't forget about the humans displaced by bank ATM machines and on-line banking. I used to enjoy chatting with young teller girls in my local bank. I accepted the fact that they were rather cold towards me due to my advanced age and hair loss. But they usually warmed up a bit once they noticed my hefty bank balance. On the other hand, the lady pharmacist at the nearby drugstore is always super friendly; unfortunately, she's going to be replaced by a pharmacy vending machine.

This all pretty much convinces me that we expendable humans are on the verge of dropping out of the picture; that is, being eliminated from large sectors of our industrialized society. Faced with this eventuality, I've come up with a sensible plan to immortalize myself.

I'm taking voice lessons and intend to be hired as the newly recorded and incredibly cordial 1-800-IRS voice that eternally says, "Thank you for calling the Internal Revenue Service; press or say one for overdue tax payments, press or say two to request forms, press or say three for employment opportunities." I suppose becoming the telephonic voice for a national appliance store would've been OK too, but not for one of those darn cable TV companies.

At any rate, I'll soon be that computer-driven human voice you hear whenever you phone the IRS, and I'm really looking forward to interacting with you. By the way, please say or press one to begin a short survey regarding this reading experience.

CHAPTER 6
Reaping Her Righteous Revenge

Diamond Hills is where I live—a really nice little subdivision. The relatively new homes have that charming Old World look, and all the yards are beautifully manicured. I've had some discussions about that with my neighbor Dexter. He's a nice enough chap, although he sure does have his share of quirks, some of which may have been caused by recent events in his life.

These days, Dexter spends a lot of time sitting on his deck out back, sipping beer and sulking about everything, despite his good fortune. His wife Ruth is a wonderful gal, way better than Dexter deserves. They "had to get married" in a bit of a rush, and so Dexter was in dire need of a job. Since Ruth is the accountant at her father's huge construction firm, she convinced Dad to hire Dexter as a manager.

Dexter, who did poorly in high school, was enthusiastic about his prospects in the construction business. He bought a sixty thousand dollar pickup truck and a cutting-edge smartphone. Dexter knew wardrobe was a key element of career success; so he bought lots of dress slacks and nice shirts with trendy logos stitched on them, and he opted for Italian leather boots instead of workbooks. He loved the sterling image he saw in the mirror.

But, due to his lack of experience and know-it-all attitude, Dexter proceeded to wreak havoc at the various construction sites. The tradespeople couldn't stand him, and customers wanted to kill him. Ruth's father was extraordinarily benevolent; he laid Dexter off instead of firing him. So, Dexter was exiled to his deck at home, collecting unemployment and constantly grumbling. In fact, upon arriving home after having been let go, he declared, "No big deal; it was just another stinking lousy job."

Meanwhile, an unmarried gal next door, by the name of Suzy, was often busy working in her beautiful yard, which included a prolific spice and vegetable garden! Speaking of beautiful, Suzy frequently caught Dexter ogling her posterior while she was bent over planting seedlings or pulling weeds. Indeed, Dexter confided in me that couldn't get the vision of her shapely behind out of his mind.

Suzy's magnificently landscaped yard and highly productive garden were her passion; in fact, she won the town's annual Best Looking Yard award. So, with her newfound reputation and MBA degree, she decided to open a big garden center, which proved to be an incredibly successful enterprise. Soon, at the insistence of a town councilwoman, she got involved in local politics and ultimately ended up as a county commissioner!

Dexter learned of Suzy's seemingly rapid rise to power, and that got wheels to start turning in his mind. He had always scoffed at her meticulously maintained yard and productive vegetable garden; his was the smarter solution: Astro turf, artificial trees, and plastic flowers. Still, Dexter sensed that this "bimbo" could somehow help him get a job. So, he swaggered over to Suzy's house and boldly suggested that she help him get a management position with the county government. She said she'd be happy to put in a good word for him.

The great news came a week later; Dexter was to interview for a management position on the county staff. He donned his one Armani suit and went in for the job interview, flaunting a new smart phone. Evidently he made the right impression because he was notified that he got the job—Wow! He celebrated by making yet another visit to his hairstylist and running his already spotless pickup truck through the carwash again. He was more than ready to manage any operation.

On Monday, Dexter met up with the human resources officer. He was then introduced to gruff and grubby Elmer who was to show Dexter how to operate a Bobcat front-end loader. Dexter was puzzled and irritated: "I thought I was hiring on as a manager." The human resources officer explained to Dexter that he'll indeed be a manager—of the county's one-man compost production facility!

By chance, lovely Suzy was lounging on her front porch when Dexter arrived back home after work. As the dirty and disillusioned man stepped out of his pristine pickup truck, Suzy yelled over to him, "How was your first day as a county manager?" Dexter's face turned beet-red as he bitterly replied, "It's just another stinking lousy job."

Soon afterwards, Dexter called me over for a couple beers out on his deck. In the middle of his sulking, he confided that he just couldn't get the vision of Suzy's vindictive smirk out of his mind.

CHAPTER 7

Struggling to Get I-T Right

I was born well before the start of the Information Age; so, I'm a very lukewarm advocate of advancements in Information Technology (a.k.a. I-T). I have to struggle awfully hard to keep up with members of the digital generation. Indeed, I've had quite a few stumbles along the blissful yellow brick road that inventors and engineers paved for us, especially in my place of employment.

As a Boy Scout, I was taught that the Morse code dot-dash sounds spelling out S.O.S. are sacred and only used in times of actual distress. Well, a fellow employee's cellphone ringtone was that very same dot-dash distress signal. When it loudly sounded off, I grabbed a fire extinguisher and went to work on him, nearly freezing his butt rock-solid.

My supervisor's first marriage was a similar misunderstanding. He told me he was missing his girlfriend a lot; so, I put my hand on his fancy desk phone and said, "Why don't you give her a ring tonight?" This infatuated chap immediately bought a ring and made a very premature trip down the aisle. He and his new bride are now permanently chained together, and they constantly bicker. Needless to say, he attributes his perpetual misery to my misunderstood encouragement.

Then came the e-mail monitoring episode in which I learned the hard way about management's legal right to intercept my office e-mails. All I did was send a short e-mail to a buddy over in another cubicle, saying that our boss is an egotistical fathead. I wish I had known that he's so thin-skinned; it took me months to find another job after he gave me the boot.

In my new job, I was given a company car that's well equipped with high tech features, including voice recognition technology. Everything was going great until I got caught up in a traffic jam and started yelling commands at the company car's dashboard. The guy in front of me thought my loud barking was directed at him. He pulled a 9mm pistol out of his glove compartment and shot my car hood full of holes. The on-scene State Trooper told my boss that I was the guy who instigated the road rage incident.

I stayed with that firm for a while longer; in fact, they even gave me a snazzy smartphone for business use. Ultimately, an innocent event proved to be my fatal downfall in that job. I was draining my bladder in the restroom and simultaneously texting a message; unfortunately, my smartphone dropped into the clogged urinal I was using. My peeved boss said that any employee who can't hang onto their smartphone while "streaming" gets a pink slip.

I eventually got myself situated in a new firm. To minimize travel expenses, video teleconferencing was a frequent activity in that new job. I quickly got the hang of using the video system, so much so that I often engaged in video flirting with a voluptuous secretary at one of our overseas offices. We didn't get too deep into risqué Anthony Weiner type activity; that's because I was quickly discovered and had to start job-hunting all over again.

Well, I was lucky enough to find yet another job. This firm was way out on the cutting edge of technology; they enjoyed the luxury of 3-D hologram meetings—"Real Virtual Presence." I wasn't so keen on meeting via that mode because faraway participants could look behind me and see my creeping bald spot. At any rate, I wasn't able to break the habit of trying to shake hands with hologram participants who weren't physically present in our conference room. My boss soon lost confidence in me…

Even though I'm searching for work again, I haven't given up on using advanced technology; in fact, I just bought a 3-D printer/scanner unit. This time I've got the right IT solution, at the right time! My grouchy mother-in-law Gretchen severely criticized me for having recently fathered a baby at my advanced age. Yet, she was adamant about flying in from the West Coast so she could hold my newly born son Waldo. As I was fiddling with my 3-D printer, I told her to just stay put where she was.

To placate Gretchen, I tucked little Waldo into the cavity of my new 3-D scanning device and hit the send button; thereby transmitting a copy of him to a 3-D printer in a business center near Gretchen's house. It was a big relief to learn that the plastic version of Waldo was immediately delivered to grumpy Gretchen. Both she and my wife are very happy about how I was finally able to capitalize on advanced technology—I'm very happy too!

CHAPTER 8

Pennies Don't Always Make Cents

My grandfather Silas is a crotchety old man, and he's currently enjoying his seventh decade of frugal living. Grandpa Silas has always been a fanatical follower of the old saying, "A penny saved is a penny earned." Indeed, he's the epitome of a cheapskate, but in one denomination only—the copper penny!

Gramps left his farm and has been living in our family home for the past few years. Residing with us doesn't cost him one red cent; instead, he takes care of household projects and "mentors" us grandkids. He keeps us extremely busy with fatiguing chores; yet, he has never paid us one thin dime, let alone one of his precious pennies. We quickly realized that Gramps is the all-time greatest role model for aspiring penny-pinchers.

Here's one small example of his miserly ways. Whenever he visits a tourist attraction, he runs a few pennies through one those machines that flatten copper coins into souvenir images. The number of pennies he transforms each year coincides with the number of names on his Christmas gift list. Obviously, there's never been any doubt as to what us grandkids will receive from that skinflint Santa each year.

Likewise, I know why townspeople here say that Gramps is a "penny wise and a pound foolish." Whenever he does go out shopping, he avoids stores that advertise prices ending in ninety-nine cents; he just can't bear to part with that many pennies. In fact, Gramps is so obsessed with the one-cent piece that he jumped for joy upon learning that his ancient Mercury Mining Company stock is worth only pennies on the dollar—more pennies!

Grandpa Silas touts himself as being an honest man. Nevertheless, I've often seen him slip his hand between the cushions of our overstuffed living room furniture, usually finding a stray penny or two each time he probed. Then there was the time he was caught stealing pennies from the courtesy change dish next to the cash register at the drugstore. The judge ruled it to be mischief and put Gramps on probation. Well, I'm pretty sure he didn't count those coins as being lucky pennies.

I've always wondered why Gramps wasn't collecting Indian head pennies; all his hoarded coins bear the image of Lincoln. So, I boldly asked him why his treasury only includes coins featuring the bearded president. He coldly replied, "I'll start saving Indian head pennies when Geronimo's face appears on Mount Rushmore." Gramps turned red when I explained that Geronimo isn't even on the penny and that he rode in Theodore Roosevelt's 1905 inaugural parade; therefore, the Chief just might join both Teddy and Abe up on that mountain someday.

Gramps wisely has his retirement pension and Social Security payments automatically deposited in our local bank. However, the bank tellers hate it when he drops by to make a withdrawal; he always demands paper-wrapped rolls of pennies as payment. One disgruntled teller really set Gramps off when he mentioned the emergence of bitcoin virtual currency. The bank lobby shook when Gramps angrily shouted: "How will people be able to buy penny candy with that?" and "Where do the words In God We Trust appear on the bitcoin?"

At any rate, Grandpa Silas has led a charmed life. It seems that everything he ever wanted came to him without too much effort on his part. The fruits of his success became apparent when my mom (Penny) and her brother (my uncle Abe) snuck a peak at Gramps will last week. They'll eventually inherit a fortune, but it'll be in the form of pennies that Gramps routinely dropped into the dried up well over at his dormant farm. That well is nearly full after sixty-plus years of dumping loads of pennies down the deep shaft.

My mom and Uncle Abe were both happily grinning about their good fortune, especially because they discovered that the monetary value of all those pennies is far less than their immense value as tons of precious recycled copper. In fact, Uncle Abe has already located a firm that will melt all the pennies down to make copper wire and tubing.

Sadly, Grandpa Silas somehow got wind of their recycle plan. When he confronted uncle Abe and my mom, it was obvious that their sinister scheme had generated strong resentment. Gramps sternly told them, "You two can do whatever is in your black hearts; however, just bear in mind that if you sell those copper coins as scrap metal, you'll never again receive pennies from heaven." Mom sheepishly turned to my frowning uncle and said, "A penny for your thoughts Abe."

CHAPTER 9

Living Forever in the Cyber Cloud

The world of Information-Technology keeps spinning faster and faster, so fast that now a cloud has been generated. Terabytes of data—to the infinite power—are stored in this nebulous computer network infrastructure called the cloud. There's little doubt that my ultimate destiny is to reside in that cloud for eternity, and I'm quite comfortable with that.

First of all, I'm not going to be another one of those naïve stiffs who paid $200,000 to be frozen solid, hoping to achieve a better life after thawing out a few decades from now. How do we even know this will work out as expected? And who's going to clean up the mess if frozen bodies start melting like ice cream cones dripping in the summer heat?

Furthermore, there won't be any dramatic Pearly Gates scenario for me when I pass away. Tennessee Ernie Ford used to sing, "Saint Peter don't you call me 'cause I can't go; I owe my soul to the Company Store." In my case, it's the Apple Store, which I've actually come to accept because it's where I bought the keys to my eternal salvation.

My computer and smartphone have allowed me to project the essence of my being into the cyber cloud. All my e-mails, tweets, Facebook postings and photo albums are out there in the cloud, not to mention my digitized medical and dental records. All my personal preferences are out there too, including shopping, dining and entertainment. But I guess that's pretty much the case with everyone in America, and for much of the world's population.

However, my latest initiative has put me a cut above all those people. I had my body laser scanned as a hologram figure that was then uploaded to cyberspace where I'll permanently reside in a cloud—the new afterlife! And I know it won't be long before others come to join me there. I wish it were going to be fascinating people like Leonardo da Vinci and Elvis Presley, or even gorgeous Marilyn Monroe. Unfortunately, those people were born too early to get aboard the digital boat that will carry "believers" to the cloud.

People I expect to see in the cyber cloud are guys like Bill Gates and Donald Trump, and maybe even Madonna. Oh yeah, guess I should have mentioned that it takes a lot of money to get uploaded to the cloud. Not to worry though, the Chinese are already busy cloning the upload software and creating a knock-off cloud infrastructure of their own; so, the cost of having your hologram uploaded will soon be mere pocket change. Fair warning though: expect lots of dragons to be wandering around their cloud, and bland rice will be the main staple.

At any rate, I'll probably be participating in quite a few séances when I start living in the cloud. They're bound to be a huge success for everyone involved. The mediums won't be the classic wide-eyed, mysterious ladies speaking in a solemn voice. Instead, computer geeks will temporarily download my hologram figure from the cloud so that séance participants can directly interact with me.

I worried all my life about whether I'll eventually ascend to glorious heaven or descend to fiery hell, the existence of which I take as a matter of faith. So, I've always stayed safely between the boundaries of good and evil, never doing anything too awfully good and never doing anything too awfully bad. Thus, I was told that I might have to spend a long time in some dark place called limbo before a final determination can be made as to my eternal destiny.

Well, all those worries are over now that I discovered the cyber cloud. These days, I can do whatever I want, with no silly accountability issues or painful consequences to fret over. The cyber cloud may not be heaven, but at least I'm not going to fry in hell.

Initially, I'll probably be a little bit lonely in the cloud, but lots of wonderful folks will join me with the passage of time and we'll all have great fun together. That is, until human nature takes its course and one of us declares himself or herself to be the sovereign ruler. Obviously, such an assertion would be viewed as a rather presumptuous act.

That being said, please tell me which one of you commoners is next in line for laser scanning to become a hologram figure.

CHAPTER 10

Dreaded Dentist Gets His Due

Now that I'm retired, my son does the quarterback hand-off to me pretty darn often, giving me lots of chores and errands to do. That said; I'm certainly happy to be driving my granddaughter Suzy to the dentist. It was no surprise to learn that her appointment is with our small town's only dentist, Dr. Yankovich. That's the guy who dragged me through the long and painful evolution of his dental practice.

Forty years ago, Dr. Yankovich was essentially the purveyor of great pain in his futile efforts to help patients. His practice was similar to what the Three Stooges set up in the Old West after attending a one-week dental school. The pain they inflicted on their patients made Spanish Inquisition torture seem like a

Sunday picnic, and they sometimes extracted the wrong tooth!

The very young Dr. Yankovich showed up here with equally questionable credentials. However, he was clever enough to establish his practice in a small office above a steak joint that was notorious for serving the toughest meat in the county. Customers would often pay for their dinners and then quickly proceed upstairs to see Dr. Yankovich.

An archaic drill was the centerpiece of the Doc's primitive office. It's grinding sound was nerve wracking, especially when accompanied by screams of anguish. Indeed, brave men cowered at the sight of his bizarre tooth extraction tools made of cold steel. Likewise, the unsightly steel braces he installed on teenagers were so bulky that kissing sweethearts often got their mouths locked together.

In the beginning, Dr. Yankovich offered me cheap whiskey or laughing gas to dull the pain— certainly nothing funny about the experience though. When he finally did start using Novocain, the needles were so thick that injections made me see stars. At the end of each visit, his receptionist always handed me a lollipop to ensure that I'd be back with more cavities.

Sadly, I eventually lost all my teeth; so, the Doc fixed me up with my first set of crude choppers. The ill-fitting dentures were extremely uncomfortable and unreliable. They sometimes fell out of my mouth while I was speaking during board meetings, and one time they went flying across the room when a young lady slapped my face in reaction to some overly aggressive flirting.

At any rate, townspeople here soon took on the likeness of an angry mob, focused on Dr. Yankovich. He hurriedly left town, headed for the state university to study both dentistry and business management. A rich uncle then bankrolled him so he could start anew. Thus, Dr. Yankovich was a changed person when he returned to our town some years later.

His new office is modern and palatial, and he keeps his luxury Mercedes parked near the entrance to reassure patients that they'll be receiving top-notch dental care. Now he uses cutting-edge technology and advanced techniques. His new drill makes a space-age whirring sound that suggests painless precision.

These days, the Doc applies invisible acrylic braces in order to ensure that teens don't inadvertently get locked together while they're necking. And his teeth whitening procedure turns homely folks into Hollywood stars. In fact, a few local gals with bright white smiles and pumped up lips have achieved the enviable status of being trophy wives.

Dr. Yankovich touts dental hygiene as essential to good health; so, no more lollipops as you exit his office. However, the Food Channel on the waiting room TV prompts patients to consume decadent deserts that rot out teeth, thereby perpetuating his dental practice. The Doc's office computer is linked to every dental insurance firm in the nation, thus allowing him to vigorously milk that herd of cash cows.

Don't get me wrong; everyone in town is pleased to see that Dr. Yankovich has transformed himself into a contemporary professional. And no one seems to resent the fact that his profitable practice allows him to enjoy a luxurious lifestyle. You know, maybe all the pain I suffered at the hands of Dr. Yankovich over the years was simply my dutiful part of helping his dentistry practice evolve into what it is today. On second thought, maybe not...

With that in mind, my granddaughter Suzy and I headed off to the dentist. While driving, I mentioned to her that there's a bag of delicious licorice candy in my car's glove compartment. Don't say it! I know I'm a despicable demon for involving my granddaughter in any sort of vengeful act, but I did it anyway.

It was obvious that Suzy really enjoyed the bag of sticky black licorice; she sure chewed up a lot of it! Indeed, she was wearing a huge black smile as the receptionist escorted her into Dr. Yankovich's office.

By the way, I think I'm pretty much finished being one of Dr. Yankovich's patients. I've got an appointment to get state-of-the-art dental implants at the Speedy Teeth drive-thru dental clinic that just opened up on the other side of town.

CHAPTER 11

Outspoken Butterfly Speaks Out

Hi there! I'm the monarch butterfly that hangs around in your back yard. I'm introducing myself in the hope that you'll begin to properly address me as Your Majesty. That's because I'm sick and tired of being called a butterfly; do you see any greasy butter or margarine on my wings? Other countries have nicer names for me—like *mariposa* in Spanish and *farfalla* in Italian. The French affectionately call me a *beautiful papillon*. But don't get confused; for them, a yellow parking ticket flapping under a windshield wiper is referred to as a *damn papillon*.

Few people are aware that I suffered an identity crisis earlier in life, back when I was a creepy caterpillar. Plus, I was worried that I'd eventually become a moth; that is, one of those dingy nighttime butterflies. Instead, I soon morphed into a regal monarch butterfly, known and admired by all. And I do enjoy all that admiration, except from the sadistic morons who try to catch me with butterfly nets so they can choke the life out of me and then mount me in a display case—C'mon people…

But let's briefly focus on my fascinating legacy. The Greeks believed an emerging butterfly was the birth of a new human soul. **Slavic people believed that butterflies were the souls of angels, making a brief visit to carry people's wishes back to heaven.** Mexicans believed butterflies to be a sign of fertility. Evidently, all our fluttering south of the border really paid off; Mexico's population rapidly grew to one hundred twenty million friendly people! But in the end, I believe the Orientals pretty much got it right, calling the butterfly a symbol of joy.

We butterflies have been associated with the world of music for many years. Giacomo Puccini's opera *Madam Butterfly* is a heartfelt testament to our popularity. The psychedelic rock group Iron Butterfly sang about us all getting high in the Garden of Eden. Then there's country music star Bob Carlisle who sang "Butterfly Kisses." Please excuse me for having to say the heck with daddy's little girl; it's clear that Bob's song is actually a touching ode to us butterflies.

Of course, we butterflies are also renowned for our athletic prowess. Even Muhammad Ali praised us: "Float like a butterfly and sting like a bee." Then there's the famous butterfly swim stroke. Truth be known, I shy away from water sports, but I do enjoy watching Olympic athletes emulate my moves. And before you scoff, consider the Canada to Mexico migration I make each year—somewhat longer than your wimpy twenty-six mile marathon run!

As you well know, we butterflies have an extremely positive Image. We're frequently featured on greeting cards and calendars. Girls love to get colorful butterfly tattoos, and they cherish butterfly jewelry. Actually, adding butterflies to any scene, even if it's ugly and tragic, makes it highly appealing to viewers. One single fluttering butterfly has more star power than a dozen floating party balloons.

Speaking of power, let's consider the butterfly effect. With just a little bit of wing flapping, I can alter the path of an emerging hurricane so that it misses you. Another boon to mankind is my hard work pollinating flowers and crops; yet, pesky bees take all the credit for doing that. I'm also a big feature of the tourism industry; people flock to the Valley of Butterflies on the Greek island of Rhodes and to the monarch roosts in Central Mexico.

But in all honesty, my life isn't pure bliss. Many predatory animals see me as nothing more than a tasty snack. In high winds, I get tossed into the gutter with the leaves. And, I have to compete with cute humming birds. You know, it's hard for me to understand why you people put out delicious nectar for them but only dried up bushes for me. Then there's the highway traffic to contend with. Many of my relatives have been wacked by speeding cars; their humiliating fate is to be a gooey blotch on the grille of an automobile that's headed to the nearest carwash.

Well, I myself have been pretty darn lucky throughout my life, but now I'm in my waning years. So, I'm just going to relax and live off of my meager Social Security checks. At this point in my life, smelling the roses will be my main pastime. Maybe you humans should consider doing the same, rather than everyone trying to kill each other to the point of extinction. You'd do well to heed advice from us butterflies. Unlike the stupid dinosaurs, we've managed to survive on this planet for over a hundred million years.

CHAPTER 12

What's Wrong With Kids Today?

In the Broadway musical "Bye, Bye Birdie," a grouchy comedian by the name of Paul Lynde posed the question: "What's the matter with kids today?" That was way back in the '60s. Strangely enough, I'm feeling equally cranky about this very same issue fifty some odd years later—something's not right here!

It all seems to start with Christmas gifts. A Tiddlywinks game and a Tonka Toy bulldozer used to round out my annual Santa experience quite nicely. Today, baseline gifting for a six-year old is a high-tech video game console and a small electric or gas powered ride-on vehicle, either a motorcycle or an ATV. Families with two or more kids have to take out a second mortgage to pay for today's obligatory gifts.

When I was a teen, I was happy with my wardrobe consisting of a few durable clothing items from J. C. Penny or Sears. Today's teens really up the ante, especially the girls. They opt for signature attire made out of thin synthetic material and manufactured in Third World sweatshops. The trendy garb is designed to be in vogue for one season only; that way, the kids can develop their power shopping skills at an early age. These days, smart kids don't leave home without a fully loaded prepaid credit card.

Speaking of money, have any of those brats thought about working for pay? I remember doing chores around the house to earn my fifty-cent weekly allowance, cutting the neighbor's grass for five bucks, and stocking shelves at the supermarket for a $1.50 an hour. Then there was the summer job where I helped bale hay, getting an arms and face "farmer's tan" as my bonus. Nowadays, youngsters ponder their dim futures while lounging in spa tanning beds.

Admittedly, they do prepare for their future by attending school. I remember being tested on longhand math and complex physics problems, each requiring a sharp pencil and two or three sheets of ruled paper to solve. Today's kids don't bother with silly longhand calculations; they've got an App to solve any complicated math or physics problem. They earn an

"A" by simply plugging in a few numbers and touching the "Solution" icon button.

Actually, the lazy way seems to be the only way today, no pressure or strain for these kids. Back-in-the-day, my generation had to stay fit because—instead of dealing with cyber bullies—we went toe-to-toe with real schoolyard bullies, sometimes suffering a black eye or fat lip in the process. Isn't this the kind of learning experience that would help today's kids become tough, street-smart leaders, ready to face global bullies like China, Russia and Iran?

Likewise, the concept of child discipline in modern times is pathetic. No more spanking with a hairbrush or belt, and no more washing the mouth out with soap. The 1-800 lawyers are extremely eager to handle any kid's lawsuit against his or her parents. All that parents have left in their arsenal today is lowering a brat's Internet speed or blocking his favorite cable TV channel. Of course, the ultimate punishment is when a parent stops chauffeuring their kid to and from school in a luxury automobile, thereby forcing him or her to ride a nerdy yellow school bus.

Truth is, my granddaughter's new boyfriend "Snoop-Azz" epitomizes what I see in kids today: hair gelled straight up, silver stud through the side of his nose, and a fierce snake tattooed around his right arm. I suppose he wears "good clothes." However, the true value off his togs is more or less thirty bucks—tie-dye T-shirt, torn jeans and plastic flip-flops. He sits around wearing wireless earphones so he can listen to cussword rap music while playing ultra violent video games.

When I eventually tried to get acquainted with Snoop-Azz, he boldly studied my facial expression and body language. Evidently he quickly perceived that I was highly stressed out over the latest developments in computer technology. He slowly removed his earphones and asked, "Hey old man, you're looking *mucho* frustrated; is there anything I can help you with?"

Well, Snoop-Azz proceeded to reprogram my flat-screen TV, getting me eight new channels. After that, he linked my bargain-basement cell phone to the car; now I can safely chat while driving. Then, in just one afternoon, Snoop-Azz built a nice website for my old-timers bocce ball club—what a whiz kid!

You know, perhaps kids weren't very kind to cranky old Paul Lynde back in the '60s, or maybe he just wasn't receptive to them. In any case, I guess things have turned around since then. Now that I've finally come to appreciate talented youngsters like Snoop-Azz, I really don't think there's anything the matter with kids today.

CHAPTER 13

Living Life With Lots Of Batteries

Italian inventor Alessandro Volta brought batteries into our lives in the year 1800. He'd certainly be shocked to learn how batteries have permeated every aspect of contemporary life, including the lithium versions created later by John Goodenough and Wilson Greatbatch. For me, this battery thing has been a cultural transformation that I strongly resisted at first but now willingly accept.

Those darn batteries have sort of emasculated the American male, as evidenced by that silly pink Energizer Bunny. Plus, much less physical energy is needed to get things done these days, and everything is done more quietly. I really miss all the traditional mechanical sounds around the house. That's all been replaced by the beeping sounds of battery-powered devices, coming at me from all directions.

All of yesteryear's macho tools seem to have evolved into high tech toys. To preserve my ego, I've kept my manly hand-crank drill even though I received a high tech battery-powered version for my birthday. Then there's my old gasoline powered lawnmower; the loud noise and blue smoke it emitted reassured everyone that I was working hard. Now I use a battery-powered mower to quietly and discretely mow the tiny patch of grass in front of my townhouse.

I also miss my old car; it had a powerful V8 that would roar through dual exhausts when I stomped on the gas pedal. I felt like King of the Road in that automobile, especially when gas station attendants swarmed the car to check its vital signs and wash the windshield. Now I've got a wimpy plug-in electric car that recharges at home in my garage—what a loss of virility! Same deal with today's battery-powered "ride-on" toy cars for kids; how are little boys going to develop into strong lads if they don't pedal those toy cars?

Shaving my face with a double-edge safety razor is another manual activity I miss. There was lots of blood and cursing at first, but through the years I honed my shaving skills to perfection. The battery-powered shaver I received last Christmas takes all the pride out of shaving. I also miss the mechanical sounds of my old rotary dial telephone—finger in the numbered holes to dial around, digit by digit. Plus, it sounded like a real telephone when it rang! Now I've got a confusing battery-powered wireless phone that stops working if I don't get it seated just right in the charging stand.

You know, winding my old Timex once a day used to be a calming experience, and that ritual allowed me a few moments to ponder the previous twenty-four hours of my life. Now, I install a wafer thin battery in my watch every few years and just carry on with my perpetually hectic life. Then there was my simple Kodak Instamatic camera that required me to manually advance the roll of film, exposure by exposure—a very gratifying activity. The insanely complicated digital camera I have now uses a small battery and takes hundreds of photos without any tending from me.

I also remember walking up to my old wood cabinet TV each time I wanted to change channels, turning the big dial one channel at a time—clunk, clunk, clunk. Now, my high tech entertainment center requires four battery-powered remotes to operate, done while siting in a "Lazy-Butt" recliner. Sadly, the candy dish on the nearby end table is now kept filled with replacement batteries instead of sweets.

Actually, the most exasperating thing about batteries is shopping for them. Every type of device uses a different size battery, and new models of the same device always use a different battery. Plus, if several manufacturers happen to make the same size battery, each gives it their own unique model number. Back in the day, battery selection was so simple; there were only a half-dozen shapes and sizes to choose from. Admittedly, they all had a tendency to leak out their chemical guts as they expired.

Obviously, the battery-powered lifestyle leaves me with sort of an empty feeling and, as you just heard, I've had very negative feelings about batteries. However, my attitude toward batteries became more positive last week. That's when a young surgeon installed my battery-powered pacemaker—a rather straightforward "bada bing, bada boom" procedure. Now my heart beats at a respectable seventy throbs per minute, and they even guarantee that it'll take a licking and keep on ticking.

All I can say at this point is, thanks very much Mr. Volta and associates. I really enjoy living life with my new pacemaker, powered by one of your nifty batteries!

CHAPTER 14

Welcome Back From Cyberspace, Children

My Grandma was prematurely banished to a senior retirement home. She was relaxing in her tiny studio apartment, sipping tea and enjoying a reread of *The Count of Monte Cristo*. Suddenly, she heard frantic knocking. What a surprise to see daughter-in-law Claudia at the door, and even more of a surprise to hear the words: "Granny, come back home—we need you!" Grandma thought to herself, "I'm not your granny, you despicable little bimbo."

Claudia continued, explaining that terrorists had detonated an electromagnetic pulse bomb, just off the East Coast. It didn't cause physical damage, but the pulse disabled every computer and digital device along the Eastern Seaboard. Grandma grabbed a few things and left with her agitated daughter-in-law who was thinking to herself, "Unbelievable, I have to drag this old witch back to *my* house."

When Grandma arrived back at the old family homestead, she saw her son and the grandkids all sitting rigid on the couch. Judging by the their blank stares, they were in a state of cyber-shock. Claudia said, "Granny, you're our only hope of getting through this crisis." The whole scenario quickly came into focus and Grandma started formulating her plan.

She knew the high tech microwave oven wouldn't work. Without those Frozen Dinner, Instant Noodle and Pizza Slice auto-cook buttons to rely on, that floozy Claudia would have absolutely no idea how to prepare the family's meals. Her first lesson will have to be how to boil water.

The kids' violent video games won't work anymore either, but they can learn to play the *Parcheesi* and *Monopoly* board games that are still up in the attic. And they may as well grab the shoebox full of old family photos while they're at it; their own smartphone photo albums reside in the cyberspace cloud that was just dissipated by the electromagnetic pulse.

Next, the kids will be whining about how the Smart TV doesn't work—no way to watch movies. Well, they'll just have to wait for the Saturday matinee at the dilapidated movie theater near here. Hmmm, besides buying the tickets, they'll need some money for popcorn and Milk Duds.

Yep, money is yet another problem. Automatic Teller Machines and the credit card network are out of service. Luckily, there's the mason jar buried ten paces west of the oak tree in the backyard—plenty of paper and coin money in the jar.

The grandkids live for their Facebook friends out in cyberspace, never mind that there are families with kids their age living in the area. They'll have to be encouraged to get somewhat familiar with folks in the neighborhood they're growing up in. By the way, it doesn't matter that landline telephones are dead. The kids normally touch a friend's name to connect via smartphones; the actual phone numbers to be dialed are long forgotten.

They're also faced with the additional problem of no texting or e-mail service. Sadly, schools stopped teaching kids how to handwrite cursive style. They'll need lessons at home so they can start sending letters via the postal service. It'll also be necessary to tutor some basic pencil-and-paper math now that their calculators and tablet computers aren't working.

A little music around the house sure would help get the family get back to normal, but they don't have any music without Internet radio streaming. Wait a minute, they can listen to old LP records on the Zenith phonograph that's out in the garage; its glass tube technology surely survived the electromagnetic pulse.

Of course, all the new cars with imbedded computers have conked out. So, it'll be necessary to jump-start the family's 1952 Mercury that's rusting away in the back yard; it'll probably run just fine. Naturally, the adults will need training on how to drive a stick shift and how to park without computer assist.

Alright then, once everyone comes out of shock, this whole family should be able to pretty much live everyday life again, albeit slightly different than what they're accustomed to. Oh, they're snapping out of it already; here come Claudia and the kids—finally smiling!

"Great news Granny! Homeland Security workers are in the process of setting up emergency Internet and cell phone services here. Next week they'll be passing out free smartphones, notebook computers, and even microwaves. So after next week, we won't need you here anymore."

Grandma replied, "That's wonderful news Claudia; meanwhile, here's an old book of fairytales for everyone to enjoy, starting with *Hansel and Gretel*. Say, perhaps we could all visit a real gingerbread house sometime soon." Claudia dryly replied, "Sure Granny, I suppose that would be fun for the kids and me." Grandma winked and said, "Yes, especially for you Claudia."

CHAPTER 15

Vanity Doesn't Stand the Test of Time

For some inexplicable reason, my aging rapidly accelerated the day I started collecting Social Security, and I found that impossible to accept. Sensing my anxiety, my wife Wanda insisted that we go down to St. Augustine and visit the Fountain of Youth. I drank gallons of their precious spring water and even bathed in it, all to no avail. After that huge disappointment, I became grouchy and difficult to live with, so much so that Wanda told me to get lost.

I kept sulking long after I moved into an efficiency apartment, but the proverbial light bulb eventually illuminated my cranium. I got together with my health care provider and quickly organized a plan of action for rebuilding me to look just as I did thirty years ago. No doubt about it, this was my one big chance to hit life's reset button. I even discovered that the Affordable Care Act covered portions of my physical renovation strategy.

The first order of business was to get a decent hairpiece to hide my baldness. Then I went for blue contact lenses, the bifocal kind. Next came dental implants from Drive-Thru Dentistry and a facial tune-up from Frank's Facelift—laughing gas from the former and painful needles from the latter. My torso makeover consisted of a brutal liposuction session, followed by application of an adhesive prosthetic for instant six-pack abs. Then came the two butt implants that beefed up my sagging rear end.

All that bodywork came with a rainbow of pills to keep me physically energized, including the most gratifying element of my former Don Juan persona. The side effects from those pills are nothing I'd care to discuss here; it suffices to say that I had to get a rental van to transport cases of adult diapers to my apartment. Not to worry; I shook off all that misery and proceeded to start living life on the wild side.

Bar hopping became my primary pastime, especially flirting with scores of cute waitresses. I favored redneck bars, including one that had a mechanical bull. There, I was able to establish an amorous—albeit superficial—relationship with a giggly cocktail waitress who was about half my age. Based on my physical appearance at the time, Cyndi-Beth seemed to be a perfect match for me. As we chatted, Cyndi-Beth hinted that she'd love to have the pretty pickup truck that was the grand prize for the bar's mechanical bull contest. My overinflated ego said, "You can do this—cowboy up!"

After having watched a few local chaps ride the bull with mixed results, I took my shot at winning that pickup truck for Cyndi-Beth. Well, I did the best I could on the bucking bull, but things quickly spun out of control. First, my hairpiece fell to the floor; then one of my blue contacts popped out. The bull's violent movement sent my cheap dental implants flying across the barroom and caused my fake six-pack abs to start peeling away from my body. The coup de grace was a violent buck that sent me flying through the air, landing on my posterior. Both my butt implants burst, leaving little to hold up my designer blue jeans.

I heard plenty of chuckling as I hobbled out of the bar. Where to now? Naturally, the prodigal son parable flashed through my mind, although it would be my wife at the door. When I arrived at the house, I rang the doorbell with one hand and held up my jeans with the other. Wanda came to door and gestured me inside. Before I walked in, I tore off the fake six-pack abs and tossed the sticky gel slab into the bushes. I was very relieved to learn that Wanda finally empathized with my male menopause crisis. Despite my disheveled and dilapidated appearance, we kissed and made up.

Shortly thereafter, I dutifully pulled together the remnants of my diminishing physical attributes in an effort to look as good as possible in my waning years. Then I started sorting through all the medical bills for the cosmetic work I had done prior to my escapades in Fantasy Land. While doing that, one thought kept racing through my guilty mind: How can I make this up to my darling Wanda?

Wanda was truly surprised and pleased when I handed her the keys to a cute pickup truck I just bought for her. At her prompting, we occasionally use it to visit an urban cowboy bar for an evening of Texas two-step dancing. Gosh, despite my advanced age, my wonderful wife and I probably could have been having this kind of fun all along. Who knew?

CHAPTER 16

Oldster Outsmarts Artificial Intelligence

After spinning for billions of years, planet earth and I finally made it to the year 2025—your future! Both Mother Earth and I are somewhat worse for the wear, although I didn't appear on the scene until the early1940s. Since that time, there's been continuous conflict between nations that has harmed mankind. On the other hand, there've been numerous technological advances that have helped mankind.

One of them is Artificial Intelligence (referred to as A-I). Its been touted as the major contributing factor that allowed mankind to finally emerge from an era of global chaos and cross-border violence. AI was the "weapon" employed by the United Nations to negotiate peace throughout the world. On a more personal level, AI has transformed my daily living.

AI is essentially a computer system capable of intelligent behavior, including learning from experience. Looking back on events, it's clear that AI was a long sought after Holy Grail, pursued by scientists for many decades. Once this technology was mastered, average people no longer needed attributes such as common sense, sound judgment, street smarts, or even proverbial horse sense.

In this new era, AI figures out everything for us and a superior intellect in humans has only minimal utility. Although I'm somewhat ambivalent about all this change, I have capitalized on AI to a certain extent, in the form of my AI-based robots dressed in spiffy uniforms.

I purchased an AI chauffer to drive me around town; thankfully, that ended my worries about passing the state drivers license exam at my advanced age. James was the name I gave to my plastic dummy filled with computer chips. James is a pleasant enough chap, although my wife is always a little embarrassed when he starts up with the off-color jokes while driving.

Truthfully, the guy is such a good driver that my auto insurance premium rates dropped way down. His only real flaw is that he's an enthusiastic sports fan who often makes unexpected, spontaneous stops in stadium parking lots, always in search of a rowdy tailgate party.

Then there's my pet robotic dog with his AI-based brain and personality. He seems loyal enough as he happily wags his synthetic tail; plus, no more outdoor potty strolls! Sadly, Fido can't fetch the newspaper because the news is no longer printed on paper, but he does exhibit some traditional dog behavior. Whenever sparks and smoke come out of his nostrils; I know he's about to start chasing our mailman.

The inevitable finally happened the other day; the mailman was found lying on the sidewalk, his blood-spattered trousers torn where my robot dog bit him. His lawyer at "1-800-Ambulance-Chaser" is trying to figure out who gets sued: the software programmer, the Robo-Pet shop, or poor old me?

We also have an automated shopping robot that sits in our computer nook 24 hours a day. He stays busy surfing the web and ordering lots of stuff based on what he has learned about our home, attire and lifestyle. Only problem is that whenever he accidently clicks on the wrong size or color, the merchandise returns are pure hell.

I'm proud that my shopping robot has the guts to stand up to bully computer systems at customer service centers as he tries to get a return authorization. But in the end, he succumbs to telephone answering trees and elevator music designed to generate frustration and confusion. So, my supposedly smart shopper usually gives up the fight, and loses my money!

Back in the day, our beloved family physician routinely said, "Take two aspirins and call me in the morning." Today, an AI-based diagnostic robot shoves probes into every orifice of my body in order to pinpoint a given malady. I suppose that's OK, but I wish this Doc had the good sense to warm up all those metal probes before insertion—Yikes!

A few years ago, he determined that I had a weak ticker and needed a pacemaker. So, he referred me to a surgical robot that performed the delicate operation. I subsequently found out that "Robo-Doc" was ogling a shapely blond O-R Nurse while installing the Timex hardware in my chest. As a result, my permanently stimulated heart is always racing.

Useless whining aside, there's no escaping the fact that AI has finally become part of our daily lives. In fact, I've come to the conclusion that AI isn't such a bad thing after all. Whenever I used to get into trouble, my wife would say to me, "You have no one to blame but yourself." These days, I can blame AI for everything that goes wrong in my life.

My clever strategy of blaming AI sure put an end to our marital spats. Wow, looks like I've finally outsmarted Artificial Intelligence!

CHAPTER 17

Yearning for Yesteryear's Grocery Stores

Gosh, I miss grocery stores of the 50's and 60's, the kind where humble grocers like Mr. Whipple—Charmin squeezer—strolled around the store and where friendly cashiers punched in prices on cash registers that emanated the original "cha-ching" sound.

I also remember the huge pyramids of precariously stacked can goods—what an art form! Plus, back in the day, each item was sold in the same aisle and on the same shelf for decades; I didn't need a GPS equipped smartphone to locate the pancake syrup each time I shopped.

Today's supermarket is an entirely different concept. It has quaint nooks reminiscent of old-world butcher and baker shops. Another nook is the fishmonger who enjoys only limited popularity, especially after the weekend when the smell of unsold fish is so overpowering. In fact, in-house florists get frustrated because the stench of expiring seafood causes flowers to wilt.

Then there's the long cereal aisle. This used to be a selection of a half-dozen brands; now it's a mind-boggling spectrum of choices. The aisle is continually packed with whimpering little brats, all pleading with their mommies to buy cereal with a toy in the box or cereal that's pure candy. On the bright side, neighborhood dentists prosper because thousands of decaying baby teeth need to be drilled and filled.

It's amazing how prices have crept up in supermarkets. The pharmacy section of my supermarket has a blood pressure monitor station. Perhaps instead of having just one monitor station, there should be one at the end of each aisle. That way, distraught shoppers would know whether to continue on to the next aisle or to take a blood pressure pill before venturing further.

Yes, there are a couple of pricey items that I crave, things like virgin olive oil and Angus beef. I no longer suffer sticker shock when I make those purchases. What does blow my mind is the price of gourmet water. I can put two gallons of gasoline in my car for the price of a six-pack of signature water. I'd even have second thoughts about buying the stuff if I were stranded in the middle of a desert.

Then again, maybe people should stop whining about high prices in supermarkets; of course, I'm assuming that farmers and ranchers are getting their rightful fair share of the profits so they too can enjoy being part of America's fading middle class. In any event, I wish that darn armored truck picking up cash receipts three times a day would stop blocking the entrance to the supermarket.

Visiting the robust Household Items section of the supermarket makes it obvious that giant home improvement stores may soon face bankruptcy. At the supermarket, I can buy hand tools, electrical components, paint rollers and, most importantly, duct tape. Thankfully, the supermarket also sells Band-Aids for the self-inflicted wounds I suffer while in the handyman mode.

Contemporary supermarkets also cater to nearly every vice by offering quality booze, fine tobacco, dirty magazines, and even lottery tickets! A guy has to ask himself, why fly out to Vegas when all the ingredients necessary for a decadent lifestyle are so close at hand? By the way, I'm told that one supermarket chain will soon feature a mini tattoo parlor in its stores, with operating hours tailored to accommodate high school students.

It's uncanny how cashier rest breaks are timed so that there's only one swamped checkout lane available when I'm ready to pay up, thereby forcing me to use a temperamental self-checkout machine. As I start wheeling my shopping cart away from there, there's usually a group of idle employees bickering about who is going to work what shift. Naturally, they do pause momentarily to smile and wish me a wonderful day.

The last time I luckily found a short checkout line, an inconsiderate customer ahead of me cashed in thirty-four coupons and meticulously balanced her checkbook for the week while my melting ice cream dripped on the floor. Likewise, I resent all the untrimmed plumage and leafs being included in my vegetable weigh-in at the register. When I complained to the produce manager, he suggested I create a compost pile in my back yard—Brilliant!

Yes indeed, I yearn for those old grocery stores that first hosted Mr. Heinz, Mrs. Butterworth and Chef Boyardee. Prices in that era were wonderful too: loaf of bread twenty-nine cents, pound of butter thirty cents, and a can of soup just ten cents. Plus, there was no competing with store employees who push wide carts down narrow aisles, urgently trying to fill multiple Internet orders for aristocrats before they arrive in their upscale SUVs to pick up the groceries.

Sure, my old grocery store wasn't a super store; it was just a really great place to shop. Mama Celeste, Granny Smith and Uncle Ben would most certainly agree!

CHAPTER 18

Paybacks for Broke Pension Funds

Hi folks! I'm Alex the school bus driver, rolling up to another of my many stops in this invigorating fall weather. I actually love my job because lots of young people benefit from it, even though many of them don't give it much thought. Oh, you may find it surprising that my full name is Alexandra—a woman of small physical stature driving a huge yellow school bus.

In fact, my husband Rodney lovingly pokes fun at me—a little lady driving a monster bus all over the countryside. That doesn't bother me; after all, transoceanic airline pilots are itty-bitty people in relation to their mammoth airplanes. Truth be known, Rodney is glad my job provides us with a little extra income. We both had great careers in the auto industry and invested heavily in pension funds. Sadly, mine was a Ponzi scheme that went up in smoke and his was tied to the housing market bubble that burst. And so now, as retirees, I'm behind the wheel of a big bus and Rodney is a cable TV installer.

My daily routine starts at 5:00 a.m. After breakfast, I commute out to the bus company yard to wake my sleeping yellow beast. I do a vehicle safety check and double-check my route while the bus is warming up. Then, I drive off into the orange dawn to pick up the first bunch of kids on my mainly rural route. They're huddled around the bus stop, chatting and laughing despite chilly weather. As I approach, I know they're only eager to enjoy the bus's warmth; even so, I hope some of them are also glad to see their smiling driver.

We roll on, bus stop to bus stop until the bus is nearly full; then it's straight to the schoolyard. I keep my eyes on the road, but I can hear what's going on as I drive. Sweethearts are whispering sweet nothings, and a bully is making intimidating threats. For their sakes, I wish they weren't oblivious to all the beauty around them as they ride: colorful autumn leaves, misty fog over the fields, and a startled fawn that's scampering to the safety of a woods. As we approach the city, hectic traffic and neon signs show the city is alive, full of spirit, and ready to receive them.

Later in the day, I return to collect my precious cargo of youngsters and drive my bus route in reverse order to drop off students, most of them tired from a long day of absorbing knowledge. Many are focused on their smartphones, exchanging romantic text messages and posting bold tweets. None of them stop to realize that they're aboard a big yellow ship that's taking them day-by-day to their future place in the world, be it a tough blue-collar job or a posh white-collar position.

Meanwhile, Rodney stays busy installing the next generation of cable TV boxes. His most recent installations have been on the ritzy side of town, where the very wealthy folks live. In fact, he mentioned that he recently installed cable boxes in the home of the guy who scammed me and the homes of crooked bank mortgage executives. By the way, those guys hired some shady lawyers and will never be prosecuted.

But in a strange twist of fate a few weeks later, the police conducted successful drug busts at the homes of the people who were responsible for the demise of our pensions. The news said the police acted on an anonymous tip. Now that's a coincidence, and a little bit of poetic justice! Hmmm, Rodney has been wearing a big smile lately, obviously beaming with satisfaction. But after thinking about it, I concluded that there's no way a meek and humble guy like him would ever engage in ruthless vengeance.

A few months later, I cheerfully waved to an oncoming bus driver behind the wheel of one of those special high-security school buses that carry prisoners to the penitentiary. I'm really glad I remembered to wave because I later learned that the prison bus was carrying that scam artist and the crooked bank executives, on their way to serve out sentences in a notoriously tough prison—not a white-collar correctional facility.

I must admit that Rodney and I are both equally pleased about those guys going to prison, no matter what the circumstances. However, I couldn't mask my surprise when he laughingly suggested that we both order personalized car license plates for those prison inmates to make. Rodney suggested that the vanity plates read: PAYBACK1 and PAYBACK2.

Oh my gosh, now that I've connected the dots, it seems apparent that my Rodney has indeed given new meaning to the old adage "Paybacks are hell." Whatta guy!

CHAPTER 19

Mysteries for 31st Century Anthropologists

Anthropology must be a truly gratifying field of endeavor. Those zealous researchers and explorers seek out the reasons for the strange traditions and behavior of ancient civilizations. Anthropologists have enjoyed a great deal of success in recent years, discovering the logic behind seemingly inexplicable actions of peoples who lived centuries before us.

For example, one Chinese emperor built an army of terracotta soldiers to accompany him on his journey to the afterworld upon his death. Of course, the Spartans tossed unwanted babies over cliffs because they appeared feeble at birth. Then there were the Polynesians who threw virgins into volcanoes in order to appease the gods.

Thankfully, the reason ancient people did those things is now pretty clear to us. On the other hand, our contemporary civilization is replete with rituals and behavior that will surely dumbfound future anthropologists, particularly because our daily actions defy all logic. Here are a dozen gems that I've been pondering:

- Praying for world peace on Sunday morning and then rushing back home to play war games on video devices linked to participants all over the globe. Let's hope our young couch potato "warriors" are just as eager whenever the military draft is reinstated.

- Converting corn into ethanol fuel for our cars even though there are millions of starving people throughout the world. Sorry poor folks; the food chain is very much broken.

- Sending men down into dangerous underground mines to extract coal for power stations so that we have enough electricity for outdoor Christmas light displays. What a pity to see Santa's little helpers all covered in black soot.

- Encouraging the fad of body piercing jewelry while, at the same time, proliferating metal detecting body scanners at airport security checkpoints. Hmm, maybe that's what forces us to be at the airport three hours early for a ninety-minute flight.

- Striving for a healthy lifestyle while enduring a barrage of nauseating medical advertisements, all trying to convince us that constant consumption of pills is our mission in life. My old Doc used to say, "Take two aspirins and call me in the morning," but only in the most dire situations.

- Hiring landscape crews to mow our lawns and then paying good money for time on a treadmill in a strip mall fitness center. Say, where are those enterprising kids of yesteryear who used to cut neighborhood lawns to make a few bucks?

- Upgrading kitchens to gourmet chef level—granite countertops and stainless steel appliances—and then only using the microwave oven or frequently ordering in fast food. Naturally, now that our white enamel appliances are gone, I'm often scolded for leaving fingerprints on the stainless steel.

- Commuting to work in a six thousand pound SUV or pickup truck even though a two hundred pound driver is the only vehicle occupant. Imagine, many of those massive vehicles cost over fifty grand, as opposed to the "$50-Junker" that used to get me to and from my town's now abandoned factory.

- Equipping chain restaurants with turbo powered air conditioners that blast out ice-cold air even though most customers wear just a T-shirt, shorts and flip-flops in the summer. Actually, an innovative restaurant chain is now giving its customers discount coupons for cold remedy medication.

- Wasting two hundred gallons of water to lounge in a hot tub while paying nearly ten dollars for a six-pack of spring water in trendy bottles. Back when I used to visit grandpa's old farm, I was comfortable using the communal tin cup hanging on the manual water pump.

- Taking blood pressure pills and calming Valium pills, and then continually watching graphic reports of killings, disasters and destruction on addictive cable TV news channels. Wish we'd get back to terse factual reporting instead of today's intentionally shocking and sexy journalism.

- Sitting down together as a family and then only communicating with each other via smartphone texts and tweets. Back when I was young, digital communications was nothing more than an obscene one-finger gesture.

At any rate, I feel somewhat obligated to help anthropologists. So, once the answers to the above mysteries become clear, I'm going to sketch informative illustrations on cave walls where future anthropologists will discover them—that's where they usually look. I'll probably etch stick men to portray our behavior, and maybe I'll even scribe a few cryptic words written in our soon to be dead cursive form of handwriting.

Look, my motives here are certainly noble enough; I just want to relieve our society of some collective guilt and make it easy for future anthropologists to look back ten centuries and understand our culture. Plus, in the process, I may even be able to create the impression that we're a highly advanced civilization, despite our incredibly illogical behavior.

CHAPTER 20

Perfection is Merely an Illusion

People continually strive for perfection, struggling to achieve it no matter what the cost. In these times of austere resources, perfection is a luxury that we can no longer afford. Instead, "good enough" and "within specifications" are standards that make more sense. Fanatics who struggle to achieve perfection are wasting time and money, and they're generating lots of unnecessary stress. Examples of this abound in our daily lives.

The Swiss brag about their handcrafted mechanical watches that supposedly keep perfect time. Other watchmakers pride themselves on timepieces that synchronize with the government's atomic clock that only loses one second in fifteen billion years. Here's the bottom line: what does it mater and who gives a damn?

That accuracy is just too much perfection, and there still remains a one-second error that couldn't be fixed!

Perfectionists that deserve a great deal of sympathy are the ones who must have everything perfectly straight—horizontal, vertical or perpendicular. For them, an art gallery visit is always a miserable experience. They can't see the beautiful artwork because they're only focused on the alignment of frames, heartbroken if they notice one that's listing one degree to the right or to the left—never mind the canvas painted by one of the great masters.

People in mild climates often boast about their perfect weather. Well, there's also perfect weather for Polar Bear Club members that break a hole in frozen ice and then jump into the lake. Likewise, fifty degrees is perfect February weather for people in the Midwest; they wear T-shirts outdoors while engaging in snowball fights. Of course, no weather at all is the perfect weather for folks who live in Tornado Alley.

There are times when you're perfectly satisfied with a purchased product or service. That's surely something to be happy about, but then you're expected to go on the Internet and visit Yelp, Angie's List, Home Advisor and the servicing company's own website to start writing rave reviews. Oftentimes, receiving fifteen minutes of satisfactory service obligates the customer to spend an hour writing perfect five-star ratings.

Fitness experts dictate to us what the perfect weight is for a given height. Well, how about the fifty-year old person who achieves the perfect weight and then proudly maintains it for ten years? Surprise, his or her shape has changed because much of that weight drops from the shoulders and chest and ends up around the waistline. This unsightly condition is what gave birth to the term "muffin-top"—a perfect description.

Of course, there's the truly perfect gift, the fruit of intense power shopping. It's always a delight to give the perfect birthday gift and then see the joy on the recipient's face and hear their profuse thanks. Problem is, that "perfect gift" rears its ugly head again on your own birthday when it's inadvertently re-gifted back to you, at which point it's no longer perfect.

The perfect balance is yet another paradox because it doesn't last very long. Scientists and technicians all strive to achieve the perfect balance. Realistically, the duration of that state is short lived; a case in point is how we routinely have to get our car tires re-balanced. Also, a ballet performer constantly maintains her perfect balance; sadly, the prima donna eventually falls flat on her derriere and then retires to run the theater's concession stand.

Say, how about the perfect response to various questions and certain situations in the workplace? For example, my cousin's boss told him that his productivity needed to significantly increase even though his paid hours were being drastically cut. His response was: "Take this job and shove it!" That was indeed the perfect answer; unfortunately, it had some pretty huge consequences for him.

Then there was the guy who was determined to commit the perfect crime. The plan was to back his truck up to an ATM machine, put a chain around the machine and hook it to his truck, and then drive forward to yank out the ATM and collect the cash. Much to his surprise, the rear bumper tore off his pickup truck when he pulled ahead. This perfectly stupid guy quickly fled the scene, forgetting that his license plate was still on the bumper he left behind.

Finally, there's the perfect marriage to consider. When people get married, they're viewed to be the perfect couple; that is, until the honeymoon is over. That's when their flaws started being revealed. My wife and I discovered plenty of flaws in each other, and we struggled with that for some years. But then we realized that it's unrealistic to expect perfection from one another and agreed to a more pragmatic approach that allows for some defects and idiosyncrasies. With that understanding, we're now perfectly happy people even though we're imperfect.

Hmm, being pragmatic seems to make perfect sense, doesn't it?

VINTAGE EXPRESSIONS

Below is a sampling of antiquated expressions. A few are still in common use to this day, while others are disappearing from the American vernacular. What an enjoyable experience it would be for seniors to educate youngsters on this quaint lingo in exchange for similar schooling on their text messaging and online chat codes. Both generations would undoubtedly enjoy lots of laughs (LOLZ) together during the tutoring sessions.

"The greatest thing since sliced bread"
"My dogs are barking"
"There's more than one way to skin a cat"
"Easy as falling off a log"
"A few bricks short of a full load"
"Put through the wringer"
"Making a mountain out of a mole hill"
"The whole nine yards"
"Low man on the totem pole"
"You can't get blood out of a turnip"
"He just fell off the boat"
"There's no such thing as a free lunch"

"Three sheets to the wind"
"Keep your nose to the grindstone"
"Sold—lock, stock and barrel"
"Something is rotten in Denmark"
"Cat got your tongue?"
"Money doesn't grow on trees"
"Raked over the coals"
"Don't throw the baby out with the bathwater"
"Katie bar the door"
"Don't cut off your tongue to spite your face"
"A day late and a dollar short"
"A bird in the hand is worth two in the bush"
"Like shooting fish in a barrel"
"Born with a silver spoon in his mouth"
"Putting on the Ritz"
"Don't take any wooden nickels"
"Trip the light fantastic"
"Pull the wool over his eyes"
"Couldn't fight his way out of a paper bag"
"Going from the frying pan into the fire"
"Caught with his hand in the cookie jar"
"I've got a bone to pick with you"
"Six of one and half a dozen of the other"
"Spare the rod and spoil the child"
"Riding the gravy train"
"The straw that broke the camel's back"
"Sixty-four thousand dollar question"

ABOUT THE AUTHOR

Retired Air Force Colonel John C. Liburdi was born and raised in Milwaukee, Wisconsin. He eagerly joined the Navy to see the world in the mid-'60s. Six years later, the sailor jumped ship and joined the Air Force to continue on with his unusually long forty-year career in uniform.

Liburdi has a bachelor's degree in psychology and a master's degree in management. He also holds professional credentials in the telecommunication and information systems field, his military specialty. During his military career, he served primarily in multiservice and multinational organizations. He served at sea and in foreign countries for twenty-nine years.

Upon retiring, Liburdi took up freelance writing. He started out addressing serious subjects in a rather serious way, but then he shifted to writing about serious subjects in a humorous way. His articles are regularly featured in senior oriented periodicals throughout the country.

9 781365 520334